Published by Moraine Book Services

404 – 2 Clarendon Avenue
Toronto, Ontario
M4V 1H9

978-0-9808904-0-2

Word | Sign | Culture | Self

A Primer on Linguistic and Semiotic Anthropology

Ivan Kalmar

Moraine Book Services
Toronto

Preface

This booklet is a revision of *Anthropological Linguistics and Semiotics,* which saw three previous Quirk editions, the last one published in 2003 as *Word, Sign, Culture*.

The booklet is meant to support a series of lectures on its various topics. It is a springboard for the lecturer and the student to explore some ideas. It is not meant to be used as reading material independently of the lectures.

The division of the text is essentially into three parts. The first is an introduction, the second a look into the fundamentals of linguistic structure, and the third an examination of the way cultures and societies are constituted in part by using not only language but also other meaning-making tools (the non-verbal codes employed in a range of activities of which a few that we mention are advertising, wine-tasting, public events). I have attempted to show how even the most minute matters of linguistic structure create and perpetuate aspects of culture and society.

My hope is that the book, if used appropriately, will lead students to explore further into the fascinating worlds of linguistic and semiotic anthropology. Just as importantly, it should compel them to find a new perspective on what might mistakenly appear as "ordinary" aspects of their everyday lives as *homo sapiens*, maker of signs.

Toronto, October 26, 2007

Chapter 1 Basic Concepts: Language and Sign

1.1 Nature and Culture

Much of anthropology is about the interaction of nature and culture in human societies. To human beings, nature appears in ways that are mediated by *representation*. Representation is part of culture: it is the way groups of people imagine the world. One way of representing the world is by means of art, another by means of writing, and yet another by means of language. These are examples of different sign systems we use to understand the world and to communicate our understanding of the world to others.

We do not know the world directly, but only through our representations of it, through language and other signs.

1.2 Language

Linguists and anthropologists study language ultimately as a universal phenomenon - the "language faculty." They are interested in particular languages such as English, Vietnamese, or Swahili as products of that universal "faculty."

There are many universal features in language. For example, all languages appear to have nouns and verbs.

This may be because we are programmed as humans to easily process only certain kind of language rules. For example, it is difficult for us to make negatives by reversing the word order in a sentence. This would mean that the negative of the sentence:

Real Finns hate electric saunas

would be

Saunas electric hate Finns real

Try to reverse the word order of any of the sentences in this book or any other sentence you can think of, in order to follow this imaginary "negative rule." You will see that this is very difficult to do.

It is difficult because our minds have not been "programmed" to process such rules easily.

In contrast, it is very easy for us to learn to place a verb after a noun. If you had to learn to reverse the typical noun-verb order in English, you would be saying:

Lost the Leafs yesterday

instead of

The Leafs lost yesterday

You would not have nearly the trouble learning such order reversal that you had when you tried to reverse the complete word order of a sentence. Try it!

1.2.1 Do not confuse language with its "channel."

Language need not be spoken. Deaf-mutes have language, but express it other than vocally.

Language is the language "faculty;" an innate ability possessed by humans. It has a structure (e.g. "nouns come before words") that is independent of the way we express it: through speech, through writing, or through sign language.

Speech, writing, and sign language are "channels" for sending language messages to others.

Alternatively, they can be labeled "codes." Speech, writing, and sign language are different ways to encode language. The person who hears or reads, or who understands sign language *decodes* language.

Many anthropologists claim that chimpanzees can to some extent "have language." They don't mean that chimpanzees can speak or write, but some chimpanzees have been taught to use and to understand human sign language. This, if true, means that they can use human language, but only in one of its *channels*.

Do not confuse language with communication. ***1.2.2***

A few decades ago the most popular way of looking at language among anthropologists and linguists was to think of its main function as communication. But language need not be communicated: internal "speech" exists, too. Consider:

a) The words and phrases we think with segment and categorize a world that might otherwise appear to us as pure chaos.

b) Part of this is that the words and phrases we think with also segment and categorize our social relationships; those between ourselves and other people.

c) Perhaps the most important way that this happens is when language helps us to segment the social world into what we call "I" (the *ego*) and others.

d) Similarly, at the group level language compels us to differentiate between our group and others, "us" and "them"

The Greeks understood some of this, as their word *logos* referred to both reason and language. In Christian theology, following both Greek and Hebrew traditions, *logos* is also the manifestation of God. In the Bible it says that God created the world through language. The Gospel of John begins as follows:

> **In the beginning there was the Word, and the Word was with God, and the Word was God.**

In the Greek original, "Word" is *logos.* Many religious people believe that the Word created the world. Religious or not, most scholars believe today that language has much to do with the formation of both the ego and of culture and society. Or, if not language then *signs*, which is a broader category that includes language as one example of a system of signs.

Language and Other Systems of Signs 1.3

Language is not the only tool used to make and to internalize interpretations of the world. *Words*, which are justifiably thought of as building blocks of language (although we will need to complicate the picture somewhat as we go on), are only one kind of *sign.* Signs are, simply put, items that stand for other items. Intuitively, we believe that the word **dog** stands for a certain kind of animal. But so does a picture of a dog, or a photograph. Certain facts are true of words that are not necessarily true of other signs, however.

Language is arbitrary and conventional (symbolic). 1.3.1

Natural language is *arbitrary.* This means there is no *necessary* connection between the sign and what it stands for.

dog **chien** **sobaka**

are the English, French, and Russian ways of referring to the same animal. Obviously, one is not a more *natural* way of referring to canines than any other. There is no *necessary* connection between these words and the animal. The dog is called **dog** or **sobaka** by *convention* only.

Signs that are arbitrary and entirely conventional are called (following the work of the semiotician Charles Pierce) *symbols*. Most words are symbols, and language is therefore for the most part a *symbolic system*.

Arguably, the "language" of color does not work in this way. If a light green color comes across as soothing, it is probably not because of some culture-specific *convention*, but because of a universal human propensity to react to it in this way.

1.3.2 Only a small part, if any, of language is iconic.

Signs that do reproduce some aspect of their referent were called *iconic* by Pierce. A picture or a photograph of a dog is iconic, as is a recording of its barking. So is a dog paw depicted on a bag of dog food. Most non-language signs are iconic.

However, there are only a few words in every language that resemble what they stand for through the way they sound. These iconic words are called *onomatopoeia*. Examples may be:

meouw-meouw **woof-woof** **splash** **bang**

Even these may not be as imitative of what they stand for as we, enculturated by our language, might think. In Japanese, the pig does not go **oink-oink** but **buu-buu**.

Many non-linguistic signs are iconic. Consider the following:

Much of language is indexical. *1.3.3*

In addition to arbitrary and iconic signs, Pierce recognized *indexical* ones (*indices* or *indexes*). An index does not reproduce any aspect of what it stands for, yet it has an existential relationship with its referent. For example, smoke is an index of fire. The relationship between smoke and fire is neither arbitrary (totally determined by *convention*) nor iconic (smoke does not look like fire).

Consider the following words:

there **this** **up** **she** **I** **you**

These words are arbitrary in the sense that any other sequence of sounds would do (**I** is **moi** in French), but they are indexical in the sense that their exact meaning is not fixed by convention.

We need to know the spatio-temporal context in order to understand what or whom they refer to.

What is important to linguistic anthropologists is that indexical terms do not simply reflect a pre-existing reality. They encode a reality that is *constituted* as we speak. **You** become **you** to me only because I address you. **Up** becomes **up** only if I find myself under it. And we have mentioned already that language also introduces the concept we label with the word, **I**.

Many non-linguistic signs are indexical. In addition to the "smoke" example above, consider:

a mole hill **the flags on Mt. Everest** **a gold chain**

1.3.4 *Linguistics as an element of semiotics.*

We see from the above that language is a system of signs, and not the only one at that.

Linguistics, the study of language, is part, in this sense, of *semiotics*, the study of all kinds of signs. *Linguistic anthropology* and *semiotic anthropology* are disciplines that study the role of signs in human culture and society, with linguistic anthropology focused on the signs of language. Because the signs of language are easier to understand, appear to be better organized, and have been studied more extensively than other signs, the study of language provides important tools for the study of signs in general. In the next few chapters we therefore turn our attention specifically to the structure of language, that is, of linguistic signs.

Chapter 2 Conversation

2.1 Internal Speech

Reason (logos) has typically been conceived of in western philosophy as a property of individual minds. Relatedly, language as a tool for understanding the world has been studied as a "device" resident in each person's mind (the mind being, usually, identified with the brain).

However, Mikhail Bakhtin argued that each individual's language derives from language as it is shared by a group.

Internal speech is *secondary to dialogue* between different individuals.

A baby learns language through conversation with others, and by hearing others converse. Monologue happens only after dialogue is *internalized.*

In this way, our understanding of the world comes from dialogue with others. It is a social understanding as much as an individual one.

One meaning of culture is "a socially shared understanding of the world." When we internalize language we also internalize culture.

The way we internalize language and culture is through the practice of exchanging messages with others. In adults, the most typical means of exchanging messages is conversation.

Traditionally, most of our use of language was in live conversation with others through the channel of speech. Since the introduction of email and text messaging, a greater proportion of our conversations is through the written channel. However, even then spoken conversation is in many ways a model. For example, we add a symbol that means "smiling face" :), to indicate that we are just "joking." In spoken conversation this would be conveyed by body motions, including smiling.

In this chapter we examine some of the conventions of live spoken conversation.

Turn Taking: Taking, Holding, and Relinquishing the Floor 2.2

How the addressee tells the speaker that he or she can hold the floor. 2.2.1

a) **the back channel**: responses by the hearer that confirm the speaker is holding the floor, such as:

uh huh **yeah** **m-hm**

b) **finishing the speaker's sentence**

c) **gaze**: addressee gazes more than the speaker; addressee's gaze confirms that the speaker is holding the floor; speaker turns gaze at addressee if he or she wants the addressee to speak, either on the back channel, or by taking over the floor.

d) **filled pause**: Geoffrey Beattier and Phil Barnard studied calls to Bell's telephone directory service. In these telephone conversations, pauses were not longer, and turn taking not more difficult, than in face-to-face conversation.

This was because the lack of opportunity to gaze was made up by the use of the "filled pause:" **ah, um, er**.

(This is different from the back channel, though the actual expressions used may be the same. What is the difference?)

2.2.2 *How the speaker signals that the addressee may take the floor.*

a) shifts in tone (drawl)
b) using a hand movement (wave or gesture)
c) interjecting a stock phrase ("you know")
d) dropping pitch or volume of voice
e) using grammatical clues, e.g. completing a sentence

How the addressee attempts to take the floor. 2.2.3

a) shifts gaze from speaker
b) uses interjections: **er, umm** (How is this different from using the same items as back channel or filled pause?)
c) interrupts (this is not "rude" if done at certain points of the speaker's turn, such as a brief pause)

The speaker's reaction. 2.2.4

Speaker "surrenders".

a) stops talking and encourages intruder
b) stops talking but does not encourage intruder
c) keeps talking until finished thought, then stops talking

Speaker refuses to "surrender".

a) raises voice
b) repeats the same sentence
c) protests explicitly, e.g. "Don't interrupt!"
d) uses a hand gesture (What gestures could be used?)

2.2.5 *The addressee refuses to take the speaker's refusal to "surrender".*

In protest against the speaker's refusal to surrender the floor, the addressee can:

a) raise pitch / volume of demand
b) interrupt at an inappropriate place (e.g. outside a pause)
c) display facial tension
d) use gestures: clenched fist on the table, etc.

2.3 Social and Cultural Differences

One U.S. study shows that women gaze at each other in conversation 38% of the time; men 23%.

This will not be true everywhere.

Gazing at a person of the opposite sex WHILE holding the floor may be interpreted as serious flirtation in North America and Northwestern Europe; not so elsewhere in Europe. In China, it is considered quite provocative.

Speakers from different cultures also differ in their *conversational strategies.*

In European and European-derived cultures, silence is perceived as a break in communication, and is normally to be avoided in the company of all but our closest intimates.

The Inuit do not traditionally find silence embarrassing. Guests come uninvited at any time. They may sit silently at the host's house even for hours, and then leave. Keeping others out of your space is not a "privacy" right among the Inuit; not speaking is.

Gender Differences 2.4

There are differences in the way men and women conduct conversation. Research on this topic is growing both in quality and quantity. Most conclusions offered by researchers are quickly challenged by others. Here are some examples, none of which are to be taken as unquestionably valid.

Report talk and Rapport talk. *2.4.1*

Deborah Tannen maintains that men's talk aims primarily to report on facts and to seek solutions to problems. Women's talk aims primarily to build rapport among the parties to the conversation.

Part of men's conversational goals is to increase their status; women are more likely to aim for the establishment of intimacy.

2.4.2 *Do men interrupt more?*

Researchers West and Zimmerman found that in general men interrupt more, but in graduate seminars, women interrupt just as much.

2.4.3 *Do women talk more?*

In research by Ann Cutler and Donna Scott, men and women said exactly the same things, but "judges" who listened (separately) to the male and female speakers thought that the women talked more. Cutler and Scott's explanations were that either:

a) a higher pitched voice seems faster, so it seems to produce more talk within the same length of time;

and / or

b) people think that any amount of time taken up by a woman speaking is a long time.

It may be, however, that women actually talk more (though this was not the case on Cutler and Scott's recordings). If so, why? (See "Differences of Speech Quantity" below.)

Differences of Conversational Style 2.5

Deborah Tannen differentiates among "high-involvement" and "low-considerateness" speakers.

High-involvement speakers, according to Tannen, produce more language, interrupt more aggressively, shift to new topics more readily; and feel that making their feelings obvious is more important than not hurting others.

High-considerateness speakers allow their conversation partners more control over the floor; and feel that not disagreeing with the other speaker is more important than making their feelings clear.

Mutual misunderstanding. *2.5.1*

High-involvement speakers consider high-considerateness speakers hypocritical.

High-considerateness speakers consider high-involvement speakers rude and aggressive.

2.6 Differences of Speech Quantity: The Power of Silence

Tannen found that high-involvement speakers were often female.

According to the philosopher Jean-Paul Sartre, argument is sometimes the strength of groups who have had to live with violence against them but were not able to counter it with violence, as was historically the case with the Jews.

Sartre's argument may also be made about women.

2.7 The Role of Context

The differences of conversational practice given above are mostly differences of form (raising one's pitch, speaking or not speaking). In language form has, of course, much to do with meaning; but meaning depends on other things as well, such as the context in which language is being used. For example, raising pitch could mean refusal to surrender the floor in one context, and a request for emotional confirmation in another.

Chapter 3 Text and Syntax

In looking at conversation, we situated language in interaction between different individuals. In recent years anthropological linguists and other scholars have found this to be the best way to advance their understanding of language. In *linguistics* proper, however (the study of the forms of which the structure of language is made), language is studied primarily not as speech *performance* – which typically takes place between individuals – but as a *competence* for speaking, which is an attribute of each human individual.

According to Noam Chomsky, who coined the terms "competence" and "performance," competence is best studied as that of an *idealized* speaker living in a homogeneous community. This eliminates any consideration of differences among different speakers and different addressees. However, it may be necessary for getting at the basic structures of language.

Without understanding those structures we cannot adequately understand *what* language is. We need to know what language is before we attempt to understand how it functions as a *cultural resource* and a *cultural product*. Consequently, we need to know some "pure" linguistics before we can turn to linguistic anthropology.

The next chapters include some – including this one – that represent for the most part a much simplified introduction to (non-anthropological) linguistics.

Text

3.1

A conversation is a “text.” Linguists and other scholars use this term to mean a. any substantially self-contained piece of language, whether written or not (ranging from someone screaming **“Fire!”** to a long book like the Bible). Even more broadly, some speak of a film or of the architecture of a city as a text. We limit our attention for now to linguistic texts.

In recent years the study of texts has made great advances. For introductory purposes, we will simplify the discussion to a few pointers about the structure of texts.

There are rules for how *strings* of words (such as sentences) can be or cannot be combined into texts. For example, a sentence like the following does not normally appear at the beginning of a text:

In fact, he did so very well.

Here, **he** and **so** refer to a person and an action that must be known to the hearer already, probably from previously mentioned sentences.

Many texts have linguistic units that define a *beginning*, a *middle*, and an *end*.

Which part of a telephone conversation is being defined by a speaker who says:

Anyway, ...
Nice weather, eh?
Well, what I'm calling about is …

3.1.1 *Formulas*

Formulas are stereotypical constructions that distinguish the parts of a text.
Beginning:

Hello, how are you?
Fine, thanks. You?
Fine. Freezing, eh?

Once upon a time …
It has been reliably reported that …
Clouseau hated reality …

Middle:

> Look here, you creep …
>
> **See there was this …**
> **Meantime, at the Hall of Evil …**
> **Now that's not all …**

End:

> **And they lived happily ever after.**
> **OK?**
> **This is Michelle Robinson, Ottawa.**
> **Oh well … Bye!**
> **I have spoken.**

Syntax 3.2

More familiar than the rules for putting together utterances to form texts, are the rules for putting together words to make utterances. For most linguists, the basic kind of utterance they study is the *sentence*. *Syntax* is the term they use to describe the study of sentence structure – the way words and phrases are combined to make sentences.

In *Jabberwocky* by Lewis Carroll, there appears to be little "real" meaning. Yet it is possible to discern some sort of meaning in the poem, because of the syntax.

'Twas brilling, and the slithy toves

Did gyre and gimble in the wabe

All mimsy were the borogoves,

and the mome raths outgrabe.

The poem sounds recognizably English though it makes little sense. In part, this is because of the few words that do make sense, like "All," "and," or "the." What helps just as much is the features that indicate that English syntax has been faithfully followed. In the first line we see that, in **slithy toves**, a word ending in **–y** precedes one ending in **–s**. An English speaker will conclude that the first is an adjective and the second a plural noun. The order "adjective then noun" is typical for English. Can you find other examples of English syntax here?

The linguist Noam Chomsky coined a famous example of a sentence that is syntactically correct (obeys the rules of syntax) but makes no sense:

Colorful ideas sleep furiously.

He called this sentence *grammatical* (linguists often use "grammar" to mean "syntax" – not the same concept as used by most school teachers!) but not *acceptable.*

Compare sentences 1) and 2):

Banana slipped Sheldon arm broke his.
Sheldon snarked the flurophile glimbo.

Sentence 1) is ungrammatical but has sense.

Sentence 2) is, not unlike Jabberwocky's, grammatical but unacceptable.

3.3 Syntax in Non-linguistic Semiotic Systems

We find syntax, that is, rules of composition, in semiotic systems that are not language.

Students sit in a designated part of the lecture room. Can you see meaning in the syntax of how they distribute themselves across the room?

Do you know the class rules of syntax for quality photography?

Cities are designed, in North America, according to a fairly predictable syntax. Can you identify it?

3.4 Syntactic Categories: Agreement

Syntax, that is to say the rules for making strings of words that form sentences, is not just a matter of word order. Language provides an indication of which words in the sentence are related, sometimes even independently of their order. Such indication is provided by *syntactic categories*: devices to show how parts of sentences are related to each other.

The most important syntactic categories express *agreement*, e.g. *number* or *gender* agreement. Examples follow:

Number agreement. **3.4.1**

English

The kitten-s drive-∅ Sheila crazy.
The kitten-∅ drive-s Sheila crazy.

The suffixes –**s** and -**∅** show, in the first sentence, that the noun and the verb agree in *number* (plural). In the second sentence, -**∅** and –**s**, the suffixes have the same form, but their meaning is different. In this case, they mean "singular." -**∅** means "plural" on a verb but singular on a noun. –**s** means "singular" on a verb but plural on the noun.

The following sentence shows how number agreement helps to show which words are related:

Do-*es* she know and do-*∅* they know that the attendant-*∅* had previously met the officer-*s*?

(The suffix we spell –**es** here is pronounced the same and means the same as –**s**). Notice how the suffixes in italics identify which form of the verb **do** is related to which noun.

Japanese
Syntactic categories do not work the same way in all languages. Japanese does not have number agreement.

> **shimizu wa koko ni imasu**
> Shimizu *wa* here *ni* is/are.
>
> **shimizu to tanaka wa koko ni imasu**
> Shimizu and Tanaka *wa* here *ni* is/are.

Regardless of the number of nouns it agrees with ("Shimizu" or "Shimizu **and** Tanaka) the form of the verb **be** is always the same (**imasu**). In Japanese the verb does not need to agree with the noun it "goes with."

(**wa** and **ni** are Japanese particles that, on the other hand, express things that are not necessarily expressed in English. They are difficult to translate and need not be translated here.)

3.4.2 Gender agreement.

Gender agreement is no more universal than number agreement. French, German, Dutch and Zulu have gender agreement. English does not.

French

Cette province est **belle.**
This province is beautiful.

Ce chapeau est **beau**.
This hat is beautiful.

A different form of "this" (**cette** – feminine, **ce** – masculine) and of "beautiful" (**belle** and **beau**, respectively) goes with different gender nouns (**province** – feminine, **chapeau** – masculine).

Syntactic ("Grammatical") Gender has nothing to do with Social/Biological Gender. ***3.4.3***

Latin

The terms "masculine" and "feminine" were invented to describe two of the three gender classes of Latin. Latin grammarians noticed that nouns like **masculus** ("man") had to be used with adjectives like **magnus** ("great"), while **femina** ("woman") had to go with **magna**.

Can you see that "great" in Latin ends in –**us** or –**a** depending on the "gender" of the noun?

Can you see that "great" in Latin ends in **–us** or **–a** depending on the "gender" of the noun?

In the case of **masculus** and **femina**, gender is a straitforward matter: the first refers to a being that is "really" masculine and the second to one that is "really" feminine. This is not the case with most nouns, in Latin or in other languages. There is nothing female about a province (Latin **provincia**, French **province**) and nothing male about a color (Latin **color**, French **couleur**). *Syntactic ("grammatical") gender has nothing to do with social or biological gender.*

This is illustrated by the following examples:

German

der Mann
the man

die Frau
the woman

das Mädchen
the girl

In German, the article **the** can have three different genders. Though **Mädchen** refers to a female being, it takes a "neuter," not "feminine" article.

Dutch

Dutch has only two genders and consequently only two forms of the article **the**: **de** and **het**. (Although traditionalist Dutch grammarians pretend, on the basis of earlier forms of the language, that there are three genders.) "Man" and "woman" are both **de**, while "girl" is **het**:

> **de** man
> the man
>
> **de** vrouw
> the woman
>
> **het** meisje
> the girl

Zulu

The Bantu languages of Africa have large numbers of genders, and these have nothing to do with maleness or femaleness. The following are examples of "gender A," "gender B," and "gender C" in Zulu (spoken in South Africa).

Gender A (example: **amafutha**)

amafutha **ami**	my fat
amafutha **akhe**	his/her fat

Gender B (example: **isihlalo**)

isihlalo **sami**	my seat
isihlalo **yakhe**	his/her seat

Gender C (example: **uukhezo**)

uukhezo **lwami**	my spoon
uukhezo **lwakhe**	his/her spoon

You should be able to see the pattern here: the forms for "my" and "his/her" differ according to the grammatical gender of the noun. These examples show how grammatical gender has nothing to do with biosocial gender: a person's fat is no more female or male than someone's seat or spoon.

Gender is an arbitrary division of nouns for the purposes of agreement – and that's all it is.

English has no (grammatical) gender. *3.4.4*

In English, adjectives and verbs do not have gender forms. To put it another way, nouns are not divided into genders with which adjectives and verbs should agree. English does not have gender.

It is true that the pronouns **he** and **she** differentiate the "gender" of nouns they refer to. But we are talking here about biosocial, not grammatical gender.

How about the fact, however, that countries, ships, cars, and such are sometimes referred to as a **she**? ("Canada has given her best sons to the war effort.")

You will find an answer to this question when we discuss *metaphor* (Ch. 5).

Chapter 4 Morphology

In the last chapter we studied the structure of the sentence (syntax). Sentences can be said to be made up of *words*. Our next task is to look at the structure of the word. The study of word structure is called *morphology*.

One might think that the word is the smallest meaningful unit of language. Not so. There are elements of the word that themselves carry meaning.

4.1 Morphemes

The following English words obviously consist of more than one unit. They can be divided as follows:

sipp ed
care ful ly
shoe s
anti dis establish ment ari an ism

In doing this, we are not dividing the above words into syllables. We are dividing them into meaningful units (though these may coincide with syllables).

The smallest meaningful units in language are called *morphemes*. Some students wonder how it can be said that **-ed** in sipp**ed** is meaningful. However, it clearly is so. If **- ed** did not add any meaning to **sip** then **sip** and **sipped** would mean the same thing.

(That the **p** doubles, by the way, is a matter of writing, an orthographic convention that is not relevant to our discussion here. We are dealing primarily with spoken, not written language. We do not add another **p** in speech, though we do in writing.)

There are many different kinds of meaning in language. Two of them are referred to as lexical and grammatical meaning. Note that **sip** has referential meaning, but **-ed** has only grammatical meaning (past time).

A special kind of morpheme is the *zero morpheme*. The zero morpheme is not pronounced at all. It is the lack of sound, so to speak, that creates the meaning here. We have already used the zero morpheme in 3.4.1 above. To take another example:

> **university**

can be more properly represented as

> **university-∅**

The zero here indicates that the word university is singular. Compare it to the plural,

universitie-s

(Again, the difference in spelling, - **university** vs. **universitie,** follows a spelling convention that has no effect on speech.)

Figuratively speaking, the singular is expressed by taking away the plural ending **s** and not substituting any sound for it.

However, since all English nouns have a -Ø ending in the singular, we often ignore it in discussing the morphemes that make up a word.

The zero ending always has only grammatical meaning.

It only makes sense to posit a -Ø ending when there is meaning in the absence of an explicit (audible or written) morpheme. You do not want to describe *universities* as *universitie-s-* **Ø,** because the absence of a morpheme after the plural suffix (-*s*) carries no meaning. You only want to put a -*Ø* suffix at the end of *university*-**Ø,** because there the *absence* of a morpheme (specifically of –*s*) is just what carries the meaning, "singular."

Morphemes and Allomorphs

4.2

Some morphemes have more than one variant.

Often one variant occurs when the morpheme is *free*, that is to say, it is a word on its own, as is the case with **sane** or **nation**. The same morphemes are pronounced differently (again, ignore spelling conventions) when found with other morphemes within the same word: in**san**ity, inter**nation**al. In this case these same morphemes **(san/sane, nation)** are *bound morphemes.*

Consider that we can also describe **sane** as ∅**-sane-**∅, and **nation** as ∅**-nation-**∅. A free morpheme can be described by the formula:

∅-________-∅

where ________ indicates the *position* of the morpheme. ∅- and -∅ ("initial zero and final zero") are the free morphemes' *context* (the *environment* in which they are found).

The bound variants of our two morphemes can be similarly described as follows:

a) **insanity** has the **san/sane** morpheme in the position
in-________-ity

Initial **in** and final **ity** are the morpheme's context.

b) **international** has the **nation** morpheme in the position
inter-________-al

The context in which the morpheme **nation** is found here is: initial **inter** and final **al**.

The variants of a morpheme (such as **san** and **sane** and the two variants of **nation**) are called *allomorphs*.

Allomorphs are *positional variants* of a morpheme. They occur in mutually exclusive positions. In our example, the mutually exclusive positions were: "between zeros" vs. "elsewhere."

In the above examples, the context that defined each allomorph's position was other morphemes. There are other examples where it is not other morphemes, but the type of sound found in the context that matters.

Consider the plural of the English noun. The following table shows some of the regularities in the way the plural is formed in different positions. Note that the form of the allomorph depends on the preceding sound alone. Again ignore spelling. The "letters" we use to describe the sounds of a language (e.g. **č, b, d**) are part of a *linguistic transcription*. We will come back to them later.

For now let us say only that **č** represents the sound that is often spelled **ch**, and **š** the sound often spelled **sh**.

Position	*Allomorph*	*Example*
č ______	-Iz	churches
j ______	-Iz	judges
š ______	-Iz	marshes
d ______	-z	rods
b ______	-z	labs
g ______	-z	hogs
t ______	-s	rats
p ______	-s	tops
k ______	-s	cooks

Affixes

4.3

The word can be divided into a *base* and its *affixes*. In the word **decriminalize**, **criminal** is the base; **de-** and **-ize** are affixes. Affixes include prefixes, suffixes, and infixes.

de / criminal / ize
prefix / BASE / suffix

Prefixes precede the base; *suffixes* follow it.

Infixes interrupt the base:

Greek

la-m-ban
'I take'

Here the base is lab 'take.' -an is a suffix. -m- means 'I' ("first person") and it is an infix.

Oregon (Native Indian language)

ho-ts-wat "non-Indians" is formed from the base **howat** "'non-Indian."

What is the meaning of the infix **-ts** - ?

Examples of "Exotic" Morphology

4.4

Inuktitut (Inuit language of the Central and Eastern Arctic)

Inuktitut has words made up of a strikingly large (theoretically infinite) number of morphemes. Its words can be, much more often than in other languages, sentences in themselves.

> **ajji liu ruti qa ruma vuq**
> same make tool have want he/she
> "He/she wants a camera"

This example is of a single word, consisting of the base **ajji,** followed by five suffixes.

Note: It is easier to translate Inuktitut words if one reads the morphemes in reverse, from the last morpheme to the first.

Chippewyan ("Chip" - native language of Alberta, etc.)

All of the suffixes on the following page express the meaning "to handle."

Suffix	Meaning
- **a**	to handle a round solid object
- **ta**	to handle a long stick-like object
- **tsu**	to handle fabric
- **dzay**	to handle a grain-like object
- **ti**	to handle a living being
- **ka**	to handle a liquid in a vessel

Chapter 5 Language, Meaning and Culture

The last example, from Chippewyan, raises some issues about language, culture, and thought. It appears that to be a Chippewyan speaker, one would have to learn to constantly pay attention to the shape of objects and to classify them in the way suggested by Chippewyan morphology, rather than in any other way. It would lead to a distinctive way of contemplating the physical universe.

It might be that abstract concepts (such as "time" or "love") are also shaped by the language we speak. This would mean that speaking a distinct language is associated with a distinct way of understanding the world. A distinct way of understanding the world, associated with a distinct group of people, is part of what we mean by "culture," one of the central concepts of anthropology.

In this chapter we interrupt our investigation of linguistic structure, to see how what we have learned so far is related to culture as a way of understanding the world.

That each language creates a different way of looking at the world is a popular idea with a long history. In the nineteenth century, it was proposed among others by the linguist Wilhelm von Humboldt and the philosopher Friedrich Nietzsche in Germany.

In North America this old idea became associated with a rather obscure fire inspector called Benjamin Lee Whorf, who was active into the nineteen forties.

The Whorf Hypothesis

5.1

Whorf wrote that when he was a fire inspector he witnessed the following incident.

> In a wood distillation plant the metal stills were insulated with a composition prepared from limestone and called at the plant "spun limestone." No attempt was made to protect this covering from excessive heat or the contact of flame. After a period of use, the fire below one of the stills spread to the "limestone," which to everyone's great surprise burned vigorously. Exposure to acetic acid fumes from the stills and converted part of the limestone (calcium carbonate) to calcium acetate. This when heated in a fire decomposes, forming inflammable acetone. Behavior that tolerated fire close to the covering was induced by use of the name "limestone," which because it ends in "-stone" implies non-combustibility.

This is example shows how, Whorf thought, having a word in a language influences the way we think of the referent of that word. But most of his work was not on words but on morphemes. For example, he noted that a native language of the American Southwest, Hopi, did not have the tense morphemes that Indo-European languages do (e.g. past tense suffixes like **–ed** in English). He concluded that therefore the Hopi did not think of time as past, present, and future. Whorf pointed out that Hopi has verbal suffixes that imply a different view of time: a cyclical one where the same period returns time and time again. In complicated ways that we cannot cover here, he used Hopi morphology to argue that the Hopi language was better suited for discussing relativistic physics, with its conflation of space and time, than were was what he called SAE (Standard Average European – languages like English, French, or Russian).

It is important to note that to Whorf differences *within* SAE were not great enough to merit discussion.

Many of Whorf's specific points have not withstood the test of time. However, the general idea, that language influences culture-specific ways of understanding the world, still stimulates debate. It is known as the *Whorf hypothesis* (or, sometimes, including a reference to Whorf's teacher Edward Sapir, as the *Sapir-Whorf* hypothesis).

5.2 Vocabulary: "Rich points"

Michael Agar is a linguist who has discussed the type of words that only competent speakers of the language can truly understand. Such words are difficult to translate. Agar calls them "rich points." He believes that for the most part translating one language into another is not a problem. Most concepts do not vary much in meaning from one language to another (and, by implication, from one culture to another). The exception are the rich points. It is they that mark important culture-specific meanings.

schmäh

is an example of a rich point, a German word Agar learned in Vienna. It expresses the view that life is not very meaningful, rather ridiculous, so it makes no sense to try to do something about it.

What would be a rich point in English? People often answer with terms of technology, expressing a prejudice according to which technology is somehow a North American preserve. In fact **television, automobile**, etc:

a) are often not English words in terms of their origin, and
b) are very easy to understand if any speaker is shown the objects they refer to, even for the first time.

Abstract terms are more difficult to translate.

A good candidate for an English rich point is the common adjective **nice**. Of course, rich points are a relative matter: a word from language A may be hard to translate to language B, but not to language C. It would probably be difficult, however, to find another language where a word covers the same meanings as the word **nice**.

Other ordinary words like **love** may be easier to translate, but might not cover exactly the same range of meanings. Some newer English words, like **cool** when it does not refer to temperature, are also good candidates for a rich point.

5.3 Metaphoric Systems

There are many elements other than simple words that may correspond to the shared world view of a group. Below are some examples of what we call *metaphoric systems:*

"Time is a commodity"

> **We've run out of time.**
> **This machine saves time.**
> **My time is valuable.**
> **Time is money.**

"Vehicles are women"

Fill'er up with regular.
She'll be good for another ten years (said about a vehicle).

"Argument is war"

Hadley destroyed Bridgman's argument.
Your claims are indefensible.
His criticism was right on target.
If you use that strategy, he'll wipe you out.

Symbolic Classifications 5.4

Many, perhaps all, cultures divide the world into large groups of referents that can be opposed to each other. In the civilizations of East Asia, distinctions are made systematically between two classes of "things" called *yin* and *yang*, respectively. Here are some examples of items in each category:

yin	**yang**
woman	**man**
moon	**earth**
passive	**active**
smooth	**rough**
plain	**mountain**
water	**rocks**

This is a kind of metaphorical system, where each element is metaphorically associated with all the others in its category. "Woman," for example, is associated with "water." Most of the associations appear to be as devoid of any special sense as the gender categories of French or Zulu (Ch. 3 – gender may perhaps reflect lost symbolic classifications, like **yin** and **yang**). But some of them certainly embody social expectations, such as the association of women with the passive and men with the active principle.

Symbolic classifications are seldom named or explicitly declared, as they are in the ***yin / yang*** system known as ***tao***. But they may exist in other languages and cultures, including English.

Try this experiment. Start with two columns labeled:

reason	**passion**

Now put one concept from each of the following pairs of concepts in one of the two columns. Use your first reaction as a member of the culture. Do not try to be "politically correct" or to otherwise censor yourself.

sun	**moon**
man	**woman**
water	**rocks**
desert	**forest**
organic	**inorganic**
machine	**human**
animal	**human**

If you compare your answers with those of others, you might find a surprising degree of agreement between your answers and theirs.

If so, then you've discovered a symbolic classification in English

Chapter 6 Phonology

We have diverted from our analysis of linguistic structure, to show how at the level of words and morphemes we can make important connections to culture and society.

This is so at each level of linguistic analysis. We will now go "below" the level of the morphology into the sound system of languages. This is an important threshold to pass. Morphemes are the smallest meaningful units of language. The units of the sound system that we are now going to look at carry no meaning in the same sense. However, they *are* associated with social meanings. How we pronounce language is an element in the way we interact with others and are perceived by them.

6.1 General

No two speakers speak the same way. This principle allows us to recognize each other as individuals.

Yet when speaker A makes an utterance, say **"Are my eggs ready?"**, all speakers of the language have the feeling that what was said is "exactly" the same as when speaker B says the same thing. (**"Hey, you got my eggs?"** means the same thing but is not "exactly the same" in terms of what was said.) When people say exactly the same thing, we say they said the same thing "word for word." But this assumes that we can tell when people said the "same word." And we can do that because, to our ears, when two people say the same word they use the same sounds.

That people use the same sounds is not literally true. It is the difference in Mom and Dad's sounds that lets you know which one of them said "Please come home." The point is that you have an unconscious and rather mysterious ability to ignore the differences between their sounds, and distil only the similarities. This ability makes you believe that Mom and Dad both began their utterance with the same sound, which we spell **p** and (in "please") followed it with the same sound, spelled **l**.

In some way, a speaker of a language can classify all the different examples of a **p** as the same thing, and all the examples of an **l** as the same thing.

Curiously, however, there are rather major variations that speakers do not notice. For example, English speakers do not notice the difference between a **p** pronounced with a little puff of air after it (linguists write this as $\mathbf{p}^{h}$) and a **p** pronounced without such a puff of air ($\mathbf{p}^{=}$). Yet both occur in English: we say $\mathbf{p}^{h}$ at the beginning of **pit**, but $\mathbf{p}^{=}$ at the beginning of spit. The difficulty we have in noticing the difference is related to the fact that in English substituting $\mathbf{p}^{=}$ for $\mathbf{p}^{h}$ does not change the meaning of a word.

In some other languages, such as Hindi-Urdu, it does. Hindi speakers hear it easily and all the time.

A part of linguistics is to study which sound distinctions are important in a language in the way that $\mathbf{p}^{h}$ and $\mathbf{p}^{=}$ are in Hindi-Urdu, but not in English. This part of linguistics is called *phonology*.

6.2 "Accent"

Making and perceiving subtle sound distinctions – in other words, understanding the phonology – is a prerequisite for speaking a language with a native "accent." (There are, however, many other relevant factors as well.) Speaking with a "foreign accent" *indexes* a speaker as not native-born. Not being native-born is an important fact in many societies such as ours. It has a serious effect on how one is perceived and treated by others. The perception others have of us as a native or non-native speaker is *internalized* by ourselves as speakers. It leads us to create an "identity" for ourselves.

"Accents" that are not foreign (e.g. a "British accent" in Canada) are not generally speaking a matter of phonology but of phonetics – the nature of the sounds used, not how distinctions are made among them. (Phonetics is treated in the next chapter.)

According to many researchers a foreign accent is inevitable if a speaker learns a language after a "critical period" that occurs between 11 and 14 years of age. Most likely, this is indeed the case but only if the language that one learns is different enough. Unusual German speakers sometimes learn English without a foreign accent, even if they only begin to be exposed to it significantly after the age of 14. It seems that Italian, Russian, or Chinese speakers can never perform the same feat.

More important to anthropologists is the fact that foreign accents, like other subtle speech variations, help to divide people into groups whose identity, formed in large measure by using language, is important in determining the roles they play in society.

Concepts Needed to Understand Phonology 6.3

Position and context. *6.3.1*

We have already investigated the concept of "position" in our look at morphology (ch. 4). Recall that in some cases, the sounds around a morpheme (its context) determine which allomorph will be used. We also mentioned that allomorphs are found in mutually exclusive positions or (which amounts to the same thing) contexts.

A similar situation occurs at the level of the sound system, although it is more difficult for us to become aware of this than of variation and position at the morphological level.

Some similar sounds or *phones* occur in mutually exclusive positions, i.e. one never occurs in the same position as the other. The trouble is that in those cases – as with the pair $\mathbf{p}^{h}$ and $\mathbf{p}^{=}$ that we just mentioned above - people may have difficulty perceiving the difference between the phones at all.

6.3.2 *Phoneme and allophone.*

Let us stay with this example. In many varieties of English:

a) $\mathbf{p}^{h}$ occurs at the beginning of stressed syllables, and
b) occurs everywhere else (for example, after **s** as in **spit**).

"Mutually exclusive contexts" here means that $\mathbf{p}^{h}$ occurs only in the position described in a), while $\mathbf{p}^{=}$ occurs only in position b).

Similar phones that are in mutually exclusive positions are said to be **allophones** of the same **phoneme.**

A phoneme is, thus, a unit of a language's sound system that may include two or more positional variants or allophones, in much the same way that a morpheme may include two or more allomorphs. The position of an allophone is always defined in terms of other sound units in its context.

This is the simplest way to define a phoneme (though it may seem daunting to some beginning students!), and a rather old-fashioned one. It will do for our purposes, however.

Each Language Imposes its own Phonology on the Sounds of its Language 6.4

We have referred to the difference in which the English and the Hindi-Urdu speaker will typically "hear" their **p** type sounds. Here is another example to illustrate how we do not hear sounds "objectively," but rather through a "filter" supplied by the phonology of our language.

In some dialects of Spanish, the sounds **d**$^{>}$ and **đ** are allophones of the phoneme, **d.** (The transcription symbol **d**$^{>}$ stands for a **d** sound that is pronounced with the tip of the tongue on the top inside part of the front teeth. **đ** stands for a sound not unlike what we spell with a **th** in **this**. For transcription symbols, see Ch. 7).

The mutually exclusive positions are as follows:

a) **đ** is found only between vowels, and
b) **d**$^{>}$ is found elsewhere.

6.5 Minimal Pairs

In English, the situation regarding **đ** is quite different. We have just said that it is spelled with **th** in a word like **this**. (Caution: there is in English a different sound that is also spelled **th**. Compare **this** and **through**. The **th** is not the same sound in each. More on this in Ch. 7.) It is NOT one of the variants of **d**. In the examples below, notice how **đ** and **d** are found in exactly the *same* position.

We are using linguistic transcription, as well as ordinary spelling, to point out inconsistencies such as where English spells the ending **ay** of **die** and of **Thy** in two different ways (**ie** and **y**), even though there is no difference in pronunciation.

Position	Examples spelling	Transcription
_______ **ay**	**d**ie, **Th**y	day, **đ**ay
_______ **ow**	**d**ough, **th**ough	dow, **đ**ow
_______ **en**	**d**en, **th**en	den, **đ**en

Finding examples like these where two phones occur in exactly the same environment is enough to prove that they are NOT allophones of the same phoneme in the language being investigated. Two words found in the same context (such as **die** and **Thy** or **den** and **then**) are called *minimal pairs*, because they differ in only one phone.

Other examples of minimal pairs in English are:

pat / bat **wine / vine** **erect / elect.**

Make sure you understand why minimal pairs are the proof that two phones are a) not in mutually exclusive positions, and so b) not positional variants and c) not allophones of the same phoneme but elements that belong to two different phonemes.

Make sure also that you understand why describing sound units as separate phonemes or as allophones has to be done in each language differently. Though *p* and *b* are separate phonemes in English, there are not so in all languages. In Arabic, for example, they are not. You cannot find two words in Arabic that make a minimal pair on the basis of the difference in pronunciation between *p* and *b*.

Chapter 7 Phonetics

Now we "descend" to an even lower level of linguistic analysis, still within the sound system. At the level of the phoneme or phonology we were looking at how languages separate sounds into distinctive units called phonemes. We saw there one illustration of the important point that culture and language have a great role in determining even such apparently natural processes as our perception of speech sounds. To complete the picture a little more, we in this chapter have a brief look at how linguists study some of the sounds "themselves," apart from the way they are classified into phonemes. The field of linguistics devoted to this kind of analysis is called *phonetics*.

7.1 Two Types of Phonetics

7.1.1 Acoustic phonetics.

Acoustic phonetics is the study of the physical properties of speech sounds, such as their characteristic frequency distributions.

Acoustic phonetics is not generally of interest to linguists and anthropologists as much as to physicists, to engineers producing synthetic voice, etc.

Articulatory phonetics. 7.1.2

Articulatory phonetics is the study of the way sounds are produced in the "vocal apparatus."

> ***Places of articulation*** are ways of allowing the spots in the human body that play a major role in producing speech sounds.
>
> ***Manners of articulation*** are ways of allowing the breath to pass through places of articulation, thereby producing sounds.

"Oscar" is an image of the oral and nasal cavities and of the larynx (throat). A version of Oscar reproduced in Appendix One.

The places of articulation as described in Oscar, together with the manner of articulation, define each speech sound of a language. All consonants and vowels of all languages can be described in terms of place and manner of articulation. The Chart of English Consonants (Appendix Two) gives the symbols used to transcribe the consonants of English, and defines the place and manner of their articulation.

Without a linguistic transcription, it would be impossible to represent the sounds of a language accurately so that **there is only one symbol per sound.**

For additional information on phonetics, consult any introductory linguistics textbook. Unfortunately, as linguists use more than one transcription system and more than one set of terms for places and manners of articulation, consulting a text may do more harm than good to some students.

7.2 Emic and Etic

There is a parallel between the "emic" units (phonemic, morphemic) on the one hand and their "etic" subunits (phones, morphs – cf. "phon*etics*") on the other. The first are units understood as such only by those who know the language. The second can be easily noted by an outsider.

A researcher will first note the etic units. Understanding the emic ones will require intensive exposure to the language.

This distinction has been useful to social and cultural anthropologists, who have extended it to descriptions of culture. An "etic" description of a culture makes all possible distinctions; an "emic" one notes those that are significant (consciously or otherwise) to the participants in the culture. If we are outsiders then only an emic description "gets us into the head" of the people participating in the culture we are studying. If we study our own culture then only an emic description makes explicit the categories of our culture that we follow, unreflectingly, in our daily lives.

The reference here is to the fact that, as we saw in the last chapter, each language has its own distinctive phonemic system: its own distinctive way of organizing the messy continuum of sounds. Similarly, each culture is imagined as having its own way of organizing experience. We will not understand a culture's way of organizing knowledge and experience unless we "learn the culture." When we learn to speak a language we must learn the distinctions it makes in the "world" of sounds. When we learn a culture we must learn the distinctions it makes in the "world" of knowledge and experience.

Chapter 8 Language and Social Identity

We are now ready to return to the major issue in linguistic and semiotic anthropology: how linguistic and other signs play a role in the production and reproduction of culture and society, and the development of the " I" (the *ego*) in the context of culture and society. We have looked at culture in Ch 5; here our focus is on society.

The difference is that the term "culture" refers to ideas and understandings, while the word "society" refers to people and connections among them. The popular use of "culture" to refer to a group of people is, from the anthropological point of view, strictly speaking wrong.

In Chapter 6 we saw that a speaker with a "foreign accent" is perceived in a distinctive way by others, and tends to internalize that perception. The speaker is assigned an identity that he or she may not otherwise develop. Immigrants may develop identities such as "Latin" or "East European," which in their country of origin either make little sense or are far less important than more specific identities (like "Chilean" or "Slovene"). One reason is the wayother people classify the immigrant's accent.

There are other, more subtle ways in which variation in the way people speak functions in creating and perpetuating social distinctions. Chief among these are ways of speaking that *index* (see 2.1.4 above) social class. Social class dialects are the best studied example of *social dialects* or *sociolects*. Others are age and gender dialects.

Standard and Non-Standard Language 8.1

Many languages, especially those spoken in or stemming from Europe, have a form that the public considers to be "correct." For example:

I'm not comin' until you call.

is considered to be the wrong way to say what is, in correct English,

I'm not coming until you call.

Yet the first sentence is no less correct than the other. It is not a mistake, like:

I'm no coming until you call.

Rather, it is a sentence that has no doubt been said many times by different people in the English-speaking world, including native speakers.

The distinction between "correct" and "incorrect" language is, very simply, a matter of tradition and more or less unconscious social class prejudice.

8.1.1 *Standard language and hegemony.*

The forms labeled “incorrect” are more common among the less privileged social strata, principally the working class. Those labeled “correct” are more characteristic of middle class speech. Language scholars avoid the terms “correct” and “incorrect” when describing variation in a language. Instead, they speak of “standard” and “non-standard” speech. Standard speech is based on upper middle class norms.

It is a half-truth that the reason working class people use more non-standard language is that they have less education than middle class people. Educational institutions do inculcate the use of the standard in their students. But middle class speakers do not need to learn it at school. It is *their* sociolect to start with.

Schools teach the middle-class sociolect to working class students, and aim to convince them that the middle-class way of speaking is “more correct.” The process whereby the socially subordinate learn unquestioning acceptance of their subordination is called *hegemony* by some scholars, following the Italian writer, Antonio Gramsci (1891-1937). Gramsci described hegemony as the

> “spontaneous” consent given by the great masses of the population to the general direction imposed on social life by the dominant fundamental group; this consent is “historically”caused by the prestige … “

… which the dominant group enjoys because of its position and function in the world of production.

The spread of the standard, and of judgments about its "correctness," is part of hegemony.

Hegemony is, however, never total. In the case of language, it *never* manages to eradicate non-standard forms completely. People resist the hegemony to some extent. They hold on to behaviors, including linguistic ones, that are not sanctioned by the hegemony.

Everyone uses some non-standard language. *8.1.2*

While hegemony fosters the use of the standard variety, there are other social forces that tend to preserve the use of the non-standard. Most non-standard language variants are used by all social strata. It is not that the upper middle class do not use them at all. They just use them less.

The following was found to be the rate of "double negative" use among Blacks in Detroit:

Upper middle class	**2%**
Lower middle class	**11%**
Upper working class	**38%**
Lower working class	**70%**

Note also that everyone, including the lower working class, uses some standard language.

The following data are about "dropping" the final –**s** of the third person singular, producing examples like:

She know. He go ever so fast.

Norwich, England

Middle Middle Class	0%
Lower Middle Class	2%
Upper Working Class	70%
Middle Working Class	87%
Lower Working Class	97%

Detroit (African Americans)

Upper Middle Class	1%
Lower Middle Class	10%
Upper Working Class	57%
Lower Working Class	71%

(Social class classifications vary from researcher to researcher. This explains the different terms for Norwich and Detroit, for the data were gathered by different linguists in each place.)

Why Non-Standard Sociolects Persist 8.2

The above data (and there is a huge amount of other information from other places all pointing in the same direction) confirm that in spite of widespread schooling non-standard forms continue to persist, and they do so among practically all speakers. The reasons for this are not very well understood.

One fact that may be relevant is that *all* speakers normally increase the standard or middle-class features in their speech on *formal occasions*, while moving in the direction of the non-standard or working-class end of the variation on *informal occasions*. (Formal occasions are speech performances which require one to pay attention to one's speech –giving a lecture, doing a job interview, etc.)

This means that even for middle class speakers non-standard, working class speech represents informality.

In addition, it represents solidarity for working class speakers.

It has been demonstrated by *sociolinguists* that people change their speech according to whom they speak to. For example, a travel agent was recorded using the highest level of standardness with clients she thought of as superior to her in social standing, and the lowest level with those she thought were below her on the same account. She used her most comfortable, "home" level, with clients she thought were of the same social status as herself.

These facts mean that a working class person is under no compunction to use the standard when speaking informally to people he or she perceives as similarly working class. Indeed, using the standard in that social context would be inappropriate and counterproductive to maintaining friendships and other solidary relations.

8.3 Gender

In addition to work on social class and social dialects, there is a large and growing literature on how men and women speak differently.

In the nineteen-seventies, Robin Lakoff was the first important linguist to write about the difference, although feminist activists who were not linguists had done so much before her.

Lakoff claimed that women were more likely to use *frivolous expressions* that would confirm them as frivolous people with no claim to power (another example of hegemony!). Examples are:

oh, dear! (where, says Lakoff, a man would exclaim **oh, shit!**)
brother!
isn't he cute?

Lakoff also claimed that women used more linguistic features that express hesitation, because they are meant to be less decisive than men – such as *tag questions* and *hesitating intonation.*

Tag questions:

It's five o'clock**, isn't it?**
You'd stop for her**, wouldn't you?**

Hesitating intonation:

When is the final?
April twenty-fifth?

There was this guy? An' he was standing at the corner? An' my aunt came by? …

More recent research has put most of Lakoff's claims in doubt. Yet important, if more complicated, differences between men and women's speech have been shown to exist. These may be more at the level of conversational strategies than of phonology or syntax.

8.4 The Linguistic Construction of Society

Early sociolinguistic research was concerned mainly with correlating linguistic and social variation. This *variationist* work still continues, but the amount of data is now so extensive and conclusive as to permit more theoretical work aimed at understanding *why* the variation takes place.

One suggestion is that knowledge of the standard represents *cultural capital* and that this is something that is sought for and competed for by social actors along with economic capital (wealth). Cultural capital is not, of course, independent of economic capital.

Together with the concept of hegemony, the concept of cultural capital is among those that have been advanced as tools in our growing understanding of how subtle phonological, syntactic, and conversational differences are indispensable to the functioning of a society characterized by social inequality.

As people use language, including its sociolectal variants, they are not just reflecting social inequality. They are *constructing* it at the same time. A living "society" could no more exist without the activity of people relating to each other than a living "language" could exist without people speaking. And people relating to each other includes people speaking to each other. In this chapter we have seen how subtle differences in the way people speak to each other maintain social differences like those of class.

Chapter 9 Culture and Freedom

Signs, including language, function not only to communicate and to create individual meanings. Through the cooperative construction and exchange of signs people create a *shared* means of making sense of their lives, which is one aspect of what we call *culture*. In contemporary societies the creation and exchange of signs takes place, to a very large extent, by commercial means. Novels, popular music, dress and make-up fashions are a few random examples of where we get out tools for understanding the world: they are bought, sold, and advertised. This means that meaning-making is in our type of society, like most other things, business.

What is the relationship of the business of meaning-making to the business of money-making, which gives it its reason to exist? This is to ask, in terms that relate to our contemporary situation, the old question of what is the relationship of culture to our practical ways of living with one another.

Society is based on unequal access to power and privilege. How is it that most people, in a peaceful and relatively harmonious society like ours, lack the power and privileges of the few, yet accept their situation without excessive grumbling, let alone violent opposition.

Depending on your political opinions, you might say that people give their consent because they realize that though our society is not perfect, it is still the best kind there is. But most social scientists and potitical philosophers believe today that society never functions entirely by rational consent.

Hegemony

9.1

One approach that has gained considerable popularity among many left and some right wing scholars (though they make different us of it) is based on Antonio Gramsci's concept of "hegemony". Gramsci (pronounced grahm-shee), whom we mentioned earlier, described hegemony as "'spontaneous' consent given by the great masses of the population to the general direction imposed on social life by the dominant fundamental group." He put 'spontaneous' in quotation marks because although the consent given is real and genuinely felt, it only appears to be coming straight from the heart of the "great masses of the population" – in fact it has been planted there by the "dominant fundamental group."

In illiberal societies, especially totalitarian ones like those under the classic communist regimes, the powerful exercise direct control over the lives and expressions of the subordinate, and those who dissent are regularly punished by the state. In liberal democratic societies such repression may not be entirely absent, but power is generally maintained by hegemony in the Gramscian sense; that is, by gaining the spontaneous consent of the people.

Another way of saying the same thing is that in liberal democratic societies power is maintained through culture. This is one reason why commercially produced culture is so important in our time, as business ("entertainment" is one of the major exports of the United States) but also as a means of forming those values and opinions that we hold "spontaneously" (without thinking), and which support the orderly functioning of society, including its inequalities.

One way in which popular culture functions to *construct* society and culture is by defining – through various types of interaction with the public such as television ratings – what is to be strived for: what constitutes glamour, or prudence, or "family values." This is especially true of television shows.

9.2 Goods as Signs

Culture is being constructed in practically every commercial transaction; even where culture is not what is directly bought and sold.

Cars, perfumes, hair styles, jeans, and even tomatoes are packaged or presented in a way that signifies something to us about ourselves and our place in society: our "image." (The word *image* is a good example of a "rich point," see Ch. 5.)

Popular culture is "made of" goods. It is a commercial culture. We do not make its products, but use them to "express ourselves." When we buy a product we accept its intended meaning (status, sex appeal, our individuality, etc.) or we might read our own meaning into it (see about the "conformity-resistance paradigm" below). Because the products we use are signs, popular culture is a culture of consuming signs.

Language consists of signs (e.g. words) as well. We have seen that the way we use linguistic signs helps to constitute social inequality. There is a standard variety of language, modeled on the usage of the more privileged groups in society. The rest of society concurs that the standard is "right" or "correct," thereby putting "hegemony" into effect. However, non-standard varieties compete with the standard and are invested with the value of solidarity.

High Culture and Popular Culture 9.3

Though the distinction was never precise and in contemporary society is becoming ever more difficult to make, it is customary to distinguish between popular culture and high culture. Popular culture is analogous to non-standard varieties. High culture could be said to be analogous to the standard. For example, opera is today the first example most people will give if asked what we mean by "high culture" (symphonic music, gallery art, a university education, and ballet are others). However, in its heyday in the nineteenth century, opera was a rather popular "mid-brow" entertainment, enthusiastically attended by "ordinary" middle-class people. Like the standard variety of language, high culture is high culture mainly not because of its inherent characteristics but because it is associated with the more prestigious elements of society and consequently carries cultural capital (a term from the work of Pierre Bourdieu).

Gramsci believed that prestige or cultural capital was one element that, because it tends to adhere to the more powerful social groups, convinces the subordinate "masses" to give their rulers their consent.

9.4 The Mass Culture Critique

Until a few decades ago, there was as almost as much consensus about the prestige of high culture as there was about the standard. A negative view of popular culture was quite wide-spread.

Those on the political right complained that it was lowering the standards of taste in society, along with moral values that those on the right usually associate with traditional cultural preferences.

Those on the left criticized popular culture as an entertainment, like the "bread and circus" of the Romans, that diverted the population from understanding its oppression and acting against it. This criticism has received the label "mass culture critique."

Criticisms of the Media 9.5

Today, more than a generation after the mass move of working-class people into the middle class that began in North America after World War II, there is much less prejudice against popular culture (with its working-class roots) than there once was, and much less respect for high culture. Many wealthy people grew up, like their parents and grandparents, as consumers of popular culture. Consequently, some forms of popular culture have acquired cultural capital that competes with the cultural capital of traditional high culture. Jazz practically belongs to high culture today, but even other forms of music, like rock and roll or country and western, enjoy more status than before. The existence of serious collectors and historians devoted to such forms of entertainment is one aspect of this development.

In these circumstances, unequivocal criticism of popular culture is less common than it once was. Generally, criticism has been deflected to the media as purveyors of valueless popular culture.

Many people believe that the media:

a) make money by imposing their trash on people worldwide, via their financial power and command of satellite etc. technology,

b) cause sexism by depicting gender and sex in sexist ways,

c) diminish people's self respect by showing only the more privileged and the more beautiful in commercials, ads, and television programs,

d) cause violence by showing too much senseless violence.

Do you agree with the following reply to the critics of the media?

a) there is no evidence for a causal link between the content of cultural products and behavior,

b) the critics arrogantly view the public as having no mind of its own: "people will watch what they're given,"

c) the critics arrogantly assume that people are unable to distinguish fiction from reality,

d) the media critics are often people with a professional stake in high culture (elite critics, professors, teachers, gallery artists) whose real message is "Give us the money and we'll make what people really should want."

The "Free Enterprise" View

9.6

Some who wish to defend the media say that no one is forced to consume what they do not want:

"You can just turn off the TV."

The media consists of businesses with business interests. If they want to sell their products they have to produce what people want. If people want trash they give them trash, if they want fine culture they give them fine culture.

Do you agree that the following are valid responses by those who disagree with the "free enterprise" view?

a) the public can choose and influence products, but not create them. The situation is similar to democratic politics. We often choose the politician we dislike the least, because there is not one that we actually want.

b) it is misleading to suggest that the media wish to appeal to the public as a whole. Television ratings, for example, are obtained by surveying the target consumer group, not the general population.

9.7 The Conformity-Resistance Paradigm

According to many academic students of popular culture today, the truth is somewhere in between the mass culture critique and the free enterprise view. They apply to popular culture studies what we might call the "conformity-resistance paradigm."

On the one hand, people do, as the mass culture critique suggests, conform to the hegemonic values of society by consuming popular culture products. Consuming them gives them a stake in consumer society and its domination by business interests. The content of many television shows and other entertainment, furthermore, does tend to spread hegemonic messages.

These messages, however, are not accepted unequivocally. People can use products to express meanings that were not intended by the producers.

A classic example occurred in the nineteen eighties, with a fashion among young people to wear deliberately ripped jeans. The meaning of an alternative, non-conforming youth life style was "inserted" by the consumers rather than the producers.

The Tommy Hilfiger line of clothing was enthusiastically adopted in the nineties by young African-Americans associated with the hip hop subculture, and then by millions of other "homies" world wide. According to rumors, the Hilfiger company was not at first pleased with this turn of event.

Eventually, the producers responded by commercializing the grass-roots initiatives of their consumers. Jean manufacturers began to make pre-ripped jeans. Designers of elite clothing adopted new designs and brand names to deliberately court the "cool" youth market.

Romance novels were once considered a trashy entertainment for housewives. By presenting submissive heroines eager to live through the exploits of a powerful and sometimes even abusive man, romance novels were said to support the mass culture critique view that popular culture induces consumers to accept a system (in this case, patriarchy) that subjugates them.
Janice Radway studied an actual group of romance readers. She found that the readers read quite a different meaning into their novels. They admired the heroine's ability to get her way with men. They enjoyed the fantasy of what they saw as sexual freedom. They were able to get some recognition for the knowledge of exotic places and historical periods that romance novels have always fostered. And some of them gained a measure of independence by obtaining from their family the right to "take off" at specified times to read their romance novel.

It may be argued that the increase in the status of the romance novel has helped in a small but meaningful way to improve the status of women. The way for this development was prepared, no doubt unwittingly, by the "ordinary" readers of romance novels.

Video games may be understood as a means for children and young people to resist the domination of adults. Adults generally are both incompetent at these games and do not understand them. Since they are unable to control the activity, it frightens them. At the same time, children and young people enjoy it as something where their abilities and their power are greater than those of their "superiors."

9.8 Resistance and Incorporation

There are many scholars who think that the conformity-resistance paradigm represents an attitude that is far too naively hopeful. They point out that even if initially some grass-roots cultural activity is a form of resistance, it soon gets neutralized by the more powerful: specifically, by

business interests who commercialize it. Such critics might suggest that when hip hop, for example, became a commercial product with major sales figures it lost its ability to capture opposition and resistance to the "power structure." This process of neutralizing dissent or resistance and turning it into a part of the functioning, existing social order is called *incorporation.*

Other scholars suggest that although all resistance is quickly incorporated in our type of society, the continuing resurgence of resisting cultural forms does create change and erodes the power structure. The most optimistic even suggest that grass roots creativity in opposition to the existing order is the very engine of history, with the powerful doing little more than incorporating such creativity. In turn, writers who profess this opinion, such as Michael Hardt and Antonio Negri, get criticized by others as hopelessly optimistic.

We are only beginning to understand that culture is the arena where much of the conflict and competition within our society gets symbolically disputed and, often, resolved. The world of culture is a world of signs. This is one reason why understanding the nature of signs – including but not limited to the best-understood kind of signs, those of language - is so important today.

“Oscar”

Appendix One

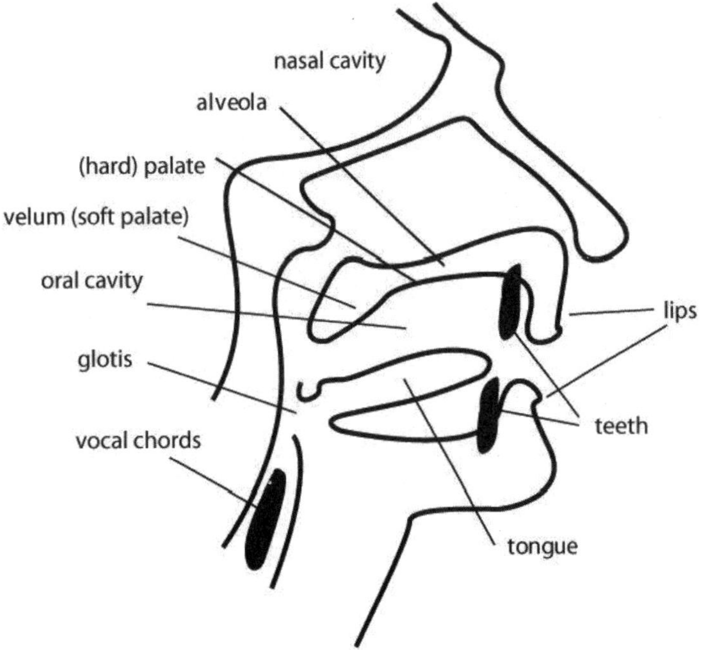

A Chart of English Consonants

Appendix Two

The classification, terms, and symbols presented here represent one common, traditional way of representing English consonants. there are many alternatives, and none has been accepted by all linguists as a universal standard.

	stop		fricative		affricatve		median	lateral	nasal	semi-vowel
	vd	vl	vd	vl	vd	vl				
bilabial	**b**	**p**							**m**	**w**
labiodental			**v**	**f**						
interdental			***đ***	**θ**						
dental/alveolar	**d**	**t**	**z**	**s**	**j**	**č**	**r**	**l**	**n**	
palatal			**ž**	**š**						**y**
velar	**g**	**k**							**η**	